Debates of Our Times

Gender Inequality

Produced by
The New York Times
in Association with
Prentice Hall

PRENTICE HALL, Englewood Cliffs, New Jersey 07632

© 1995 by Prentice-Hall, Inc.
A Simon & Schuster Company
Englewood Cliffs, New Jersey 07632

All rights reserved. No part of this book may be
reproduced, in any form or by any means,
without permission in writing from the publisher.

Printed in the United States of America
10 9 8 7 6 5 4 3 2 1

ISBN 0-13-366097-4

PRENTICE-HALL INTERNATIONAL (UK) LIMITED, *London*
PRENTICE-HALL OF AUSTRALIA PTY. LIMITED, *Sydney*
PRENTICE-Hall CANADA INC., *Toronto*
PRENTICE-HALL HISPANOAMERICANA, S.A., *Mexico*
PRENTICE-HALL OF INDIA PRIVATE LIMITED, *New Delhi*
PRENTICE-HALL OF JAPAN, INC., *Tokyo*
SIMON & SCHUSTER ASIA PTE. LTD., *Singapore*
EDITORA PRENTICE-HALL DO BRASIL, LTDA., *Rio de Janeiro*

Contents

Introduction v

No Cookie-Cutter Mothers in the 90s
By Susan Chira   1

Traditional Family Favored by Boys, Not Girls, Poll Says
By Tamar Lewin   5

Generals Oppose Combat by Women
By Eric Schmitt   11

Vatican Fights Plan to Bolster Role of Women
By Alan Cowell   13

Court, 9–0, Makes Sex Harassment Easier to Prove
By Linda Greenhouse   16

Simpson Case Is Galvanizing U.S. about Domestic Abuse
By Jane Gross   20

Women Doing Crime, Women Doing Time
By Clifford Krauss   24

Push to Revamp Ideal for American Fathers
By Susan Chira   27

Pentagon Must Reinstate Nurse Who Declared She Is a Lesbian
By Eric Schmitt   31

Women in Colombia Move to Job Forefront
By James Brooke   34

Discussion Questions 39

Introduction

Gender inequality is a new social problem in the sense that, through most of this nation's history, very few people, male or female, have publicly acknowledged that women were being treated unfairly. Although there was an important feminist movement in the nineteenth and early twentieth centuries that ultimately succeeded in securing the right for women to vote, there was very little organized feminist activity between 1920 and the late 1960s, and as a result most people today think of gender inequality as a distinctly modern social issue.

On the other hand, from a broader historical perspective, sexism is the oldest of all types of structured social inequality. Most preindustrial societies are highly culturally homogeneous, limiting the extent of racial and ethnic inequality, and many display less extreme class variations than are characteristic of modern societies, but gender inequality is built into all but the very simplest hunting and gathering cultures. This fact led Friedrich Engels to conclude that the oppression of women was the original pattern on which all other types of inequality were subsequently modeled.

The first two readings of Debates of Our Times: Gender Inequality introduce the issue of gender inequality. "No Cookie-Cutter Mothers in the 90s" overviews a wide range of the issues confronting women today while "Traditional Family Favored by Boys, Not Girls, Poll Says" documents some of the widespread attitudinal factors that make change in this area difficult to achieve.

The next four articles illustrate a variety of current issues facing women in modern society, including their role in the military ("Generals Oppose Combat by Women") and the church ("Vatican Fights Plan to Bolster Role of Women,"), sexual harassment ("Court, 9–0, Makes Sex Harassment Easier to Prove"), and family violence ("Simpson Case Is Galvanizing U.S. about Domestic Abuse").

"Women Doing Crime, Women Doing Time" suggests that, as women gain increased social equality, they are also becoming more involved in historically male problems such as crime.

The next two readings deal with gender role issues that affect men ("Push to Revamp Ideal for American Fathers") and homosexuals ("Pentagon Must Reinstate Nurse Who Declared She Is a Lesbian").

The final article introduces a cross-cultural perspective. "Women in Colombia Move to Job Forefront" explores the status of women in a Third World nation.

NO COOKIE-CUTTER MOTHERS IN THE 90s
By Susan Chira

At the American Greetings card shop at 40th Street and Broadway a few days ago, throngs of shoppers stood paralyzed in the aisles, frozen in a pre-Mother's Day panic. So many cards, so many messages, and so many of them mixed. Who is Mother anyway?

A bedrock idea is quaking, and the seismic shocks are still rumbling.

Despite the collective sentimentality and familiar homilies of this annual celebration, there is now, as seldom before, intense confusion and anxiety about motherhood. Once, it was clear what a mother was supposed to be. But now a mother can be working outside the home, or not; married, divorced or single by choice; a biological parent, an adoptive one or a recipient of donated eggs. Women can look to Tipper Gore or Hillary Rodham Clinton, women of the same generation who chose different paths. Donna Reed has given way to Roseanne, and audiences cheer "Serial Mom" as a manic sendup of the 1950s icon perkily kills people who threaten her children.

Cultural Anxiety "There is great cultural anxiety about motherhood today," said Barbara Dafoe Whitehead, who wrote "Dan Quayle Was Right," a much-debated article speaking against the rise of single-parent families, published in The Atlantic Monthly last year. "One of the reasons is that women individually have to invent this for themselves. There is no clear normative pattern."

The soul-searching about motherhood extends from the personal to the political. Report after report in recent years has offered bleak portraits of the state of American children and documented the poor quality of much American child care. Yet, scientific research has proven that the first three years of life determine the structure of the brain and forge lasting emotional patterns.

Whose Care Counts? Experts and commentators offer conflicting guidance. Penelope Leach, whose baby-care books have sold millions of copies, argues in her new book *Children First* (Knopf) that young children need individual attention, and she criticizes every form of substitute care for failing to measure up to the devotion of a mother or a father. Other child-care experts cite dozens of studies showing that for most children it seemed to make no difference in their development whether they were cared for by their mothers or someone else.

Now, there are as many definitions of the good mother as there are kinds of mothers. But what has not changed is the passion that the ideal of motherhood evokes, and the zeal with which people advance their views.

For many, Mother remains synonymous with self-sacrifice. "I think that when your kids understand consistently that you put them first, that constitutes good mothering," said Ms. Whitehead, who said she used that principle with her own children.

Unrealistic Standards But feminists in particular have tried to carve out a new definition, arguing that the traditional ideal held out an unrealistic standard of perfection and that a self-fulfilled mother has more to offer her children. They say women have unfairly borne sole responsibility for child-rearing, and call on fathers to do their part.

"The good-enough mother is one who takes care of herself so that she has something to give," said Marie Wilson, an author of *Mother Daughter Revolution* (Addison-Wesley, 1993) and a mother of five. "She doesn't take all the blame on herself. She invites men to take their share." But for many mothers, the old images die hard, although more than half of the women with children under a year old are now in the work force. "The ghost of the perfect mother is still riding on her shoulder," said Betty Friedan, who gave voice to women's demands for change with *The Feminine Mystique* in 1963. "A lot of the guilt is unnecessary. It's vestigial, from the feminine mystique added to the inappropriate 'supercareer woman' model. I think we haven't caught up with the differences."

Image of Supermom There are few new cultural icons of motherhood to take the place of the 1950s television mother. For a time in the late 1970s and early 1980s, mothers were bombarded with the image of Supermom, the woman who effortlessly combined career and motherhood. A United Airlines commercial showed a mother with briefcase in hand dropping off her child at school, hopping a plane to dazzle her clients in a business meeting, and zipping back in time to pick up her child at the end of the day.

That image proved unsustainable. And true to the increasing diversity of families and mothers, no single model has emerged to take its place. Advertisers who once enshrined mothers as happy vacuumers and floor waxers no longer speak with a single voice, offering images of working mothers, stay-at-home mothers and even fathers bathing children. "Advertisers are so afraid of offending their best customers," said Barbara Lippert, the advertising critic for Adweek magazine. "If they show mothers staying at home, the working mothers tune out. If they show them as frantic working mothers, the stay-at-home mothers tune out."

A Slight Spin Perhaps the most traditional images now in advertising, she said, are the "Dr. Mom" advertisements for cough medicine, in which the mother soothes a sick child. Even some familiar images have a slight spin, like the commercial for Jif peanut butter that portrays a mother almost as the chief executive of the home, juggling important decisions like which peanut butter to choose.

But Ms. Lippert said that advertisers still tended to stumble when they portray working mothers. "There's an ad for a birth-control pill that shows a woman sitting at a computer with her 4-year-old on her lap," she said. "This seems to say this woman is so frantic she has no separate time for her child." The closest modern analogue of Donna Reed, at least for some mothers, may be Roseanne, the writer Barbara Ehrenreich said. She continued: "It's a working-class family. She works. She's genuinely interested in those kids. She finds ways to get them to talk about the hard things without invading their space."

Defining the Good Parent Whatever their ideal of motherhood, experts, including mothers themselves, agree on what makes a good parent: someone genuinely interested in children, responsible and responsive, who endows children with sound moral values and enables them to engage in productive work and loving relationships.

The question that haunts many parents today is this: Can a mother who returns to work while her child is an infant produce such a paragon?

In a social experiment still too young to yield decisive empirical results, most mothers cling to the evidence of their experience.

A Three-Hour Limit "My kids got dropped off at day care, and one is now finishing up at Brown, and the other went through Harvard and Oxford," Ms. Ehrenreich said. "One thing I realized when my children were small was that I was a perfect mother for about three hours—imaginative, empathetic, full of activities—but longer than that, I was no good. I have no question that values were transmitted even though we were working most of the time. I'd be doing housework, and I'd give them a rag. That's when you teach them how to lead a good life, how to clean a sink." But doubts continue to plague many mothers, particularly if their mothers did not work or if they must work to pay the bills. Heidi Brennan, a co-director of Mothers at Home, a support group in Vienna, Va., said: "It is not useful to define the conflict over what is a good mother by whether you work or are at home. But I think you cannot deny your children a certain amount of hours—unless the child has a very permanent substitute, in which case the child will be more tied up with that substitute." Mothers, no matter what their personal views, tend to agree on solutions: more flexible work hours, longer paid parental leaves after childbirth, more help from fathers, more money for higher-quality child care, part-time work with benefits, and changes in the career ladder to accommodate mothers who want to curtail their hours.

Asking the Impossible But Ms. Wilson, who is president of the Ms. Foundation for Women, offered a broader critique, arguing that the traditional ideal of motherhood essentially asked the impossible: that mothers bring up children by themselves. "You can't do mothering alone," she said. Instead, she proposed that mothers actively seek out "other mothers"—fathers, family, friends, neighbors—to share the responsibility.

Black mothers have long relied on such help because so many had to work, said Janie Victoria Ward, a professor of education and human services at Simmons College in Boston.

Because children have so many different needs that are usually impossible for one person to fill, it may be advantageous for several people to help raise a child, said Lawrence Aber, a developmental psychologist at Columbia University. "If you have a couple of adults with different developmental histories, the chances of getting something right for the child at different stages go up."

A Separate Domestic Sphere Indeed, the idea that a mother's primary job was to rear her children alone at home came into its own in the 19th century, when the workplace moved from home and field to factory and the idea of a separate domestic sphere emerged, said Natalie Davis, a Princeton University historian who specializes in family history. Before then, most women worked at home alongside their husbands, and many women, even those of modest means, relied on the help of servants and extended family.

Moreover, the image of a suburban mother at home with her brood never reflected the reality for many Americans. "Most black people don't even begin to think about mothering" as incompatible with working, said Bell Hooks, a feminist writer. "We just don't see any model for that."

The current generation of Americans is caught between the old, contested image of motherhood and a new, bewildering diversity. But there are signs that mothers, whether employed or at home, do not all buy the relentless standard of perfection that most Mother's Day cards celebrate but that some movies now mock.

John Waters, the director of "Serial Mom," said, "I was raised to believe that 'Father Knows Best' was exactly how reality was." So he created "Serial Mom," a devoted suburban housewife, perfectly coiffed, entirely perverse: she's a serial killer.

" 'Serial Mom' is certainly based on how I was brought up to believe in this ridiculously perfect family," Mr. Waters said. "People are still in mental institutions because of those images they tried to live up to." (Copyright © 1994 *The New York Times*)

TRADITIONAL FAMILY FAVORED BY BOYS, NOT GIRLS, POLL SAYS
By Tamar Lewin

A nationwide poll of teen-agers found that boys are substantially more traditional than girls in their expectations of the family life they will have as adults.

The girls surveyed were more likely than the boys to say that they could have a happy life even if they did not marry and that they would consider becoming a single parent. And 86 percent of the girls said they expected to work outside the home while married, while only 7 percent said they did not.

Among the boys, 58 percent said they expected their wives to work outside the home and 19 percent said they expected their wives to stay home.

A majority of the boys surveyed said that most of the boys they knew considered themselves better than girls. But most of the girls surveyed said the girls they knew saw boys as equals.

The telephone poll of 1,055 teen-agers aged 13 to 17 was conducted by *The New York Times* and CBS News from May 26 to June 1 and has a margin of sampling error of plus or minus three percentage points.

In follow-up telephone interviews with participants in the survey, the sex differences were pronounced.

Many of the boys said they still believed strongly in a traditional 1950s-style marriage, in which the wife stays home, rears the children, cleans the house and does the cooking, while the husband is responsible for making the money and mowing the lawn.

"I think girls should do the cooking and cleaning because they're better at it, and boys should do the yard work and the planting," said Breton Stout, 15, of Clovis, Calif. "I know a lot of girls think it's real sexist to say they belong in the kitchen, and they think we should kick in on cleaning, but I think they're wrong. It's not a boy's job."

'The Wife Should Stay Home' Seventy-one percent of the teen-agers surveyed had mothers employed outside the home, and 80 percent had fathers employed outside the home. But the belief that a 1950s-style marriage is the natural order seems to have a firm hold, even among many teen-age boys whose mothers work outside the home.

"I think the wife should stay home," said Timmy Tomlinson, 14, of Hot Springs Village, Ark. "A mother should teach children what she wants to teach, not what the baby sitter wants to teach. Most of the girls around here, and in the South, are old-fashioned. They want to stay home with the kids."

There was little difference in the boys' and girls' answers to a question asking whether, in the long run, it is better for children to have a parent at home: a majority of both sexes said it was better if one parent stayed home.

Most of the girls interviewed were adamant about their plans to have a career and an egalitarian marriage. And many of the boys expressed firm convictions that a woman's place was in the home.

Committed to Careers "I'd rather my wife stayed home," said David Wells, 17, of Mineral Wells, Tex. "Why? So I wouldn't have to do the cleaning. I do yard work. I have five sisters and they do the house cleaning. They don't ask me because they know I wouldn't do it. My mom is a nurse, and she's gone from 5:30 A.M. to 5 P.M. My mom likes to work; she's always worked. But I wouldn't choose someone like that for my wife. She nags a lot, and I think it's because she's bound to be stressed out from working."

The girls surveyed, however, were overwhelmingly committed to having careers—and far less so to making and maintaining a marriage.

"I think a career is the most important thing, then children, then marriage," said Nicole Leesnan, 16, of Atlanta, Ill. "I've always wanted to succeed in a work field, maybe something like being a marine biologist. I know I will work. If I get married, I would want it to be with someone who did as much of the housework as me. I think girls are more liberated and guys are going to have to compromise. If they say they want their wives at home, I think it's because they want more power in the relationship."

Nicole, like 55 percent of the girls surveyed, said she would consider becoming a single parent if she did not marry.

"If I weren't married, I could imagine being a single mother," she said. "I know it's hard, but it's worth it. I just know I want children."

Marriage? Yes. Divorce? No While more than 9 of 10 boys and girls surveyed said they thought it was likely that they would marry and have children—and more than 6 of 10 said it was not at all likely they would ever get divorced—the girls were less likely than the boys to say they would feel they were missing part of what they needed for a happy life if they did not marry, or if they divorced.

The girls were also more likely than the boys to say that children were better off if their parents divorced rather than remained married and fought a lot.

"If I were 30 and not married, I might feel a little funny around friends that were," said Amy Hughes, 13, of Albuquerque, N.M., "but then I'd go to work and have a nice apartment that wouldn't be all messy, and I wouldn't have to share the bathroom. I admire women who don't let men get in their way. When boys say their wives will have to stay home, I think it's because they want to be the king of the house, they think it's manly."

Many of the girls said their mothers had encouraged them to be self-sufficient.

"I would never stay home and be a housewife," said Johanna Petree, 18, of Modesto, Calif. "My mom thinks I should work, every woman should, in case you get divorced and can't support yourself. My mom always worked part time at little jobs and then she went back to college and last year started teaching. I want to get a doctorate. And I want to have my career be more important to me than hers was to her."

'Husbands Are a Big Pain' Johanna said that while her father cooked every day, her mother still did more of the work around the home. And in many families she knows, Johanna said, the wife does all the work—an arrangement she would not accept.

"If my husband doesn't do it, I won't either," she said. "No one really wants to cook or clean. Men don't want to take on the roles of women, even though women have taken on the roles of men. My parents used to argue about who did the housework, but then they got a housekeeper. My mother tells me not to get married, partly joking, but I think partly serious, because husbands are a big pain. It's a lot of work keeping a relationship together, and I think women do more of the work. I'm not going to go looking for a husband just to get married. If it happens, fine." Johanna said she believed that men would change someday and take on a more equal share of the load.

"Men will have to change, to keep up with women," she said. "If men don't involve themselves with things around the house, women won't marry them. They'll wait and find someone who will."

Avoiding Housework While girls like Johanna expect their husbands to take over part of the "second shift"—the work of managing a home—many of the boys seem committed to avoiding it. And

8

even those who say they are open to sharing the housework equally, and marrying a woman with a career, seem to have some sense that there are men's jobs and women's jobs.

Nick Newland, 15, of Tiffin, Ohio, said that he would expect to work out job and household arrangements depending on what his wife wanted, and how much money he made.

"I could imagine my wife working, and my doing half the housework," he said. But for now, he mows the lawn and his younger sister cooks. "Sometimes I say, 'Why don't you mow the lawn?' and she says, 'That's a man's job.' And sometimes she says, 'Why don't you cook?' and I say, 'Because that's a woman's job.' "

Teen-Agers and Sex Roles

	All	Girls	Boys
In today's society, there are more advantages in:			
Being a man	35%	37%	32%
Being a woman	7	8	6
It's the same	55	52	59
Do most girls you know think of boys as:			
Equals	50%	57%	41%
Better than themselves	49	42	56
Do most boys you know think of girls as:			
Equals	36%	34%	39%
Lesser than themselves	61	63	59
How likely is it that you will get married?			
Very likely	63%	65%	62%
Somewhat likely	32	29	34
Not at all likely	4	6	3

	All	Girls	Boys
How likely is it that you will have children?			
Very likely	55%	57%	53%
Somewhat likely	38	35	41
Not at all likely	6	7	4
Could you have a happy life or would you feel you missed part of what you need to be happy if:			
You don't get married?			
Missed	32%	26%	38%
Still happy	67	73	61
You don't have children?			
Missed	48%	49%	47%
Still happy	51	50	52
You get divorced?			
Missed	30%	22%	37%
Still happy	68	77	60

Power of Money Amber Wilson, 16, of Oxnard, Calif., said she and her boyfriend of four years had frequently discussed their expectations of family life—and always disagreed.

"He says he should work and I could work part time," she said. "I don't know why, but he always says that would be better. I might stay home for a month or so with a baby, but I want to have a full-time job. And I expect my husband would do the same amount of work around the house I would. We never agree. We just stop talking about it."

Laquita Brown, 14, of Chesapeake, Va., said she was not sure whether she would be a nurse, a child care worker or a cosmetologist. But she was certain that she would work outside the home.

"If someone is making the money of the household, they're going to expect you to do what they say," she said. "Anyway, I want more experiences than a housewife has. And I don't have any problem with the idea of leaving babies with a baby sitter. I think it's kind of a tradition for boys to want their wife to be a housewife. But when all those boys who want their wives to stay home get married to all these girls who want to work, there's going to be a whole lot of fights." (Copyright © 1994 *The New York Times*)

GENERALS OPPOSE COMBAT BY WOMEN
By Eric Schmitt
Special to The New York Times

WASHINGTON, June 16—Senior Army generals have forced the civilian Army Secretary to retreat from an ambitious plan to open thousands of combat positions that are now closed to women.

The opposition was so great that Secretary Togo D. West Jr. has withdrawn his recommendations to Defense Secretary William J. Perry and is now huddling with the angry officers to work out a compromise.

At the heart of the clash is a confidential "decision memorandum," dated June 1, from Mr. West to Mr. Perry that recommended that women be allowed to serve in the battalion headquarters of combat engineer, air defense and field artillery units. Mr. West also urged that women be allowed to fly helicopters carrying special-operations troops and to serve as crew members of a barrage artillery system. "Readiness will improve because we will have a larger pool of quality soldiers from which to draw to fill critical jobs," Mr. West said in the memo.

The nine-page memo had barely hit the desk of Mr. Perry's top aides when the Army Chief of Staff, Gen. Gordon R. Sullivan, hit the roof, protesting that Mr. West's proposal went far beyond what field commanders had thought prudent. Many generals believe that women cannot handle the physical rigors of service in the infantry, armor and artillery, the military's most lethal ground units and the forces most likely to engage in direct combat. The generals also believe that women in those units would cause problems with morale and privacy.

General Sullivan, Mr. West and their top aides are putting the finishing touches on a revised plan that will probably open many new positions to women, but not as many as Mr. West originally proposed. The final recommendations must be approved by Mr. Perry.

The emotional issue has led customarily collegial Army leaders to snipe at each other over the way the matter has been handled. Army officers grumble that Army civilian officials recommended changes to Mr. Perry beyond what Mr. West and General Sullivan had privately settled on. Civilian Army officials say the generals were fully consulted, and the civilians suggest the officers may have misunderstood Mr. West's plan.

Few subjects are more sensitive in today's military than the integration of women into battlefield units. The performance of 41,000 women in the Persian Gulf war, from flying helicopters to driving fuel trucks, quieted many skeptics and prompted Congress to lift bans on women flying combat aircraft and serving aboard warships, leaving the policy now in the hands of the Pentagon.

But the Army and the Marine Corps remain the last bastions of most all-male units, and they have fought hard to keep women out of infantry, armor, artillery and special-forces units.

In January, then Defense Secretary Les Aspin moved to open more ground-combat jobs to women by lifting a Pentagon rule barring women from certain military jobs simply because those jobs were dangerous.

Aspin's Rule   Mr. Aspin replaced the rule with a new, three-part definition of ground combat: women are barred from units that engage the enemy on the ground with weapons, are exposed to hostile fire and have a "high probability of direct physical contact with the personnel of a hostile force." Mr. Aspin ordered the services to report by May 1 which units could be opened to women.

Most jobs in the Navy and Air Force are now open to women. Even the Marine Corps, which has only 4 percent women, plans to open 33 previously closed fields, mostly airplane and helicopter maintenance jobs and headquarters positions, a senior Defense Department official said.

But some generals are recommending that, at least for now, no more jobs be opened beyond the 7,000 additional positions in about half a dozen areas that the Army announced in January could be filled by women on active duty.

"We need to pause and let this sort out for a while," Gen. J. H. Binford Peay 3d, the Army's vice chief of staff, told the Senate Armed

Services Committee today. "We should not look at the definitions in the last Aspin directive with that kind of clinical and hygienic precision. That's not the battlefield."

Large portions of Mr. West's memo have been published in trade publications and elsewhere, putting the Secretary in an awkward spot if the final recommendations fall short of his original plan.

In an interview this week, Mr. West refused to comment on his memo or on the circumstances surrounding its withdrawal. But he discussed the process that he and the Army's personnel chief, Sara E. Lister, had used to evaluate opening new positions.

'Two Basic Principles' "The review started with taking the new rule, understanding it and measuring our positions carefully against it," Mr. West said, referring to the new definition of ground combat. "I'm fairly comfortable that measurement has taken place. But the uniformed military has to put it into operation. We're now talking about how they conduct their business in the field."

"Even the uniformed Army agrees that we have two basic principles operating here," Mr. West said. "One, everyone in this country is entitled to an opportunity to serve and should be given that opportunity. And two, the Army is a war-fighting entity that exists to fight and win the nation's wars. So the question is how to best utilize the available resources to do the latter with the least compromise of the former." The most controversial recommendations in Mr. West's memo included allowing women to operate an artillery weapon, the Multiple-Launch Rocket System, and to pilot helicopters that ferry special forces into combat, often behind enemy lines. (Copyright © 1994 *The New York Times*)

VATICAN FIGHTS PLAN TO BOLSTER ROLE OF WOMEN
By Alan Cowell
Special to The New York Times

ROME, June 14—The cardinals of the Roman Catholic Church voted today to oppose what they portrayed as a pervasive feminist influence at a forthcoming United Nations population conference, saying measures on abortion and women's rights sponsored by the United States reflected "cultural imperialism."

An extraordinary gathering of 114 of the 139 cardinals warned that the measures would legitimize "abortion on demand, sexual promiscuity and distorted notions of the family."

During planning in April for the population conference, the proposals gained broad support after Administration officials, feminist groups and many population experts emphasized that women should take prominent roles in population programs.

Proposals drafted during the talks in April also say population growth cannot be contained without expanding health services and education for women.

In a reversal from the last population conference, 10 years ago, the current draft does not explicitly rule out abortion as a woman's right. This element has drawn some of the fiercest attacks by the Vatican, which has long opposed abortion and artificial birth control.

In recent months, the Vatican has begun a campaign in countries that will send delegates to Cairo for the September talks, and Pope John Paul II has denounced the measures. The issue reportedly remained contentious in the meeting earlier this month between President Clinton and the Pope in Rome.

The cardinals' unanimous vote today, in response to an appeal by John Cardinal O'Connor of New York, further defined the battlelines. The cardinals had been called to Rome by the Pope to discuss preparations for Christianity's second millennium.

The Vatican disputes the suggestion by conference organizers that the proposals would elevate the standing of women. Vatican officials say the church prefers to promote its own concept of women as deserving equality and special respect, but within the context of church tradition.

"This conference could be of enormous value to all peoples of the world if it focuses on the family—the family, that is, in the traditional and natural sense of the word," Cardinal O'Connor said. But, he went on, "the failed social policies of many developed countries should not be foisted on the world's poor."

"Neither the Cairo conference nor any other forum should lend itself to cultural imperialism or to ideologies that isolate the human person in a self-enclosed universe wherein abortion on demand, sexual promiscuity and distorted notions of the family are proclaimed as human rights or proposed as ideals for the young," the Cardinal said.

An Eye on the Americans The Vatican's choice of the New York Cardinal to sound the alarm apparently reflected the view that much of the language that the church finds offensive comes from American feminists.

In specific terms, the Vatican fears that some draft language will weaken the family as society's most basic social and moral arbiter, lead to abortion on demand and spread access to contraception, all in direct contravention of church dogma.

For example, the draft states that "countries should remove legal, regulatory and social barriers to sexual and reproductive health information and care for adolescents." It also says the privacy of teenagers should be respected.

In the United States, supporters of the draft said the language on women's rights would not be as harmful as the Vatican supposes.

Focus on Abortion "We have no quarrel with the Vatican," said Timothy E. Wirth, the State Department Counselor. "Our purpose is to create as strong a program as possible to focus on the issue of population stabilization and on the issue of women."

Mr. Wirth said that neither the United States nor the United Nations endorses abortion as a method of family planning, but that abortion should be safe and legal. "We do not believe that a woman should be coerced to have an abortion or coerced to have a child," he said.

The draft plan mentions abortion specifically only in a chapter about the public health problems of unsafe abortions, which kill an estimated 250,000 women a year.

Several population groups said that far from being an American cause, the emphasis on women's rights reflected the concerns of women in developing nations who have been victims of forced sterilization or who have had more children than they wanted because they were subservient to men, had little formal schooling or had no access to contraception.

Response from Supporters "The agenda of this document is far broader than in the past," said Joan Dunlop, president of the International Women's Health Coalition, a private group that works with women in developing countries. "The Vatican's inflammatory language is a smoke screen; they are threatened by women having a say in their own lives."

Sally Ethelston, a spokeswoman for Population Action International, another private population group, said: "Women should not die or suffer irreparable physical harm as a result of unsafe abortions because of a group of 114 celibate men."

Even before the three-week preparatory conference in New York, the Pope went to extraordinary lengths to oppose the proposals, calling President Clinton by telephone to discuss it and personally reprimanding the conference's secretary general, Dr. Nafis Sadik of Pakistan.

In March the Pope sent letters to heads of state, seeking to persuade them that it is not the United Nations' job to lay down moral principles under the guise of population policy.

"Why is the Pope so concerned?" said one Vatican official. "This conference is very different from previous population conferences. It is basically about a type of libertine, individualistic life style, and it would be the first time the United Nations would endorse this life style."

The Pope has won some backing in Europe and Latin America, while Islamic countries have voiced aversion to the emphasis on equality of women, particularly in sexual matters.

"It would be a mistake to say that the Vatican is alone in its opposition to the draft U.N. document, that it's the Vatican that's the voice of dissent," Raymond L. Flynn, the United States Ambassador to the Vatican, said in a recent interview.

But, Mr. Flynn said, at the Cairo conference "other countries are going to have to make a choice whether to support the U.N. position or the Vatican position."

The conference is to lay down guidelines for the next 20 years on how governments deal with population growth. The current population is estimated at 5.7 billion and could rise to 10 billion within the next two decades. (Copyright © 1994 *The New York Times*)

COURT, 9-0, MAKES SEX HARASSMENT EASIER TO PROVE
By Linda Greenhouse
Special to The New York Times

WASHINGTON, November 9—Ruling with surprising speed and unanimity, the Supreme Court today announced a broad definition of sexual harassment in the workplace that will enable workers to win suits without having to prove that the offensive behavior left them psychologically damaged or unable to do their jobs.

In an opinion by Justice Sandra Day O'Connor, the Court rejected a standard adopted by several lower Federal courts that required plaintiffs to show that sexual harassment made the workplace environment so hostile as to cause them "severe psychological injury."

While psychological harm is one factor among many that courts may weigh in a sexual harassment case, Justice O'Connor said, the protection of Federal law "comes into play before the harassing conduct leads to a nervous breakdown."

'Hostile' Environment Invoking the "broad rule of workplace equality" that she said was inherent in the Federal law against job discrimination, Justice O'Connor said the law as applied to sexual harassment was violated when, for any of a variety of reasons, "the environment would reasonably be perceived, and is perceived, as hostile or abusive." She added that "no single factor is required."

The decision, only the Court's second on the subject of sexual harassment, revived a lawsuit against a Nashville truck leasing company by a woman who worked there as a manager.

For more than two years before she quit her job, the woman, Teresa Harris, was subjected to repeated sexual innuendos and demeaning comments from the company's president, Charles Hardy. For example, Mr. Hardy asked her in front of other employees whether she had obtained a particular account by having sex with the client.

Behavior Described as Inane The Federal District Court in Nashville described Mr. Hardy's behavior as "vulgar" and "inane," finding it offensive both to Ms. Harris and to a hypothetical "reasonable woman." But that court ruled against Ms. Harris on the ground that the comments were not likely to "seriously affect" her "psychological well-being."

The United States Court of Appeals for the Sixth Circuit, in Cincinnati, which had adopted the psychological injury test for sexual harassment several years earlier, affirmed the decision in 1992.

In overturning that ruling today, only four weeks after hearing the arguments, the Supreme Court's decision itself left a number of questions unanswered, and it is almost certainly not the Court's last word on the subject of sexual harassment.

It remains to be seen, for example, how lower court judges will evaluate the "reasonable person" standard the Justices adopted. While women's groups uniformly praised today's ruling, several of them had argued in friend of the court briefs against requiring sexual harassment plaintiffs to show that the conduct that offended them would also offend a "reasonable person" or a "reasonable woman." One brief, from the Women's Legal Defense Fund and the National Women's Law Center, described the reasonable person standard as "a powerful engine of the status quo." Even so, Marcia Greenberger, co-president of the National Women's Law Center, called the decision "a big win for women."

Ms. Greenberger said the Court was sending "as clear a signal as could be to employers that sexual harassment is a serious violation of the law and that the time for strained legal arguments is over." She said she hoped that lower courts would apply the reasonable person standard "fairly."

Steven R. Shapiro, general counsel for the American Civil Liberties Union, said today that the Court had made a good choice between what he called the "two extremes" of requiring proof of psychological damage on the one hand, and treating "merely offensive speech" as sexual harassment on the other hand. "It's clear that the Court takes sexual harassment seriously as an appropriate concern of Federal law," he said.

A Civil Rights Provision   The Federal law at issue in the case was Title VII of the Civil Rights Act of 1964, which bars discrimination in the workplace on the basis of race, sex, religion, and national origin. In 1986, the Court for the first time interpreted Title VII to cover sexual harassment, ruling in a 9-to-0 opinion by Chief Justice William H. Rehnquist that sexual harassment that was so pervasive as to create a hostile or abusive work environment is a form of sex discrimination.

The Court's language in that decision, *Meritor Savings Bank* v. *Vinson,* was so general that it gave the lower courts relatively little guidance in how to apply it. Today the Court interpreted the 1986 decision broadly, making it a more useful tool for plaintiffs.

For example, Justice O'Connor said that the earlier decision's reference to the emotional and psychological stability of workers, and its use of phrases like "heavily polluted with discrimination," were meant to "present some especially egregious examples of harassment" and "do not mark the boundary of what is actionable." One of the most important parts of today's opinion, *Harris v. Forklift Systems, Inc.*, No. 92-1168, was its rejection of a requirement that the plaintiff's job performance actually suffered. Some employer groups had argued for this standard. But Justice O'Connor said there was no need for a plaintiff to prove this or any other "tangible effects" from harassment.

Justice O'Connor said the definition of sexual harassment "by its nature cannot be a mathematically precise test." Rather, she said, courts should look at "all the circumstances" to determine whether a work environment is a hostile one.

These circumstances may include "the frequency of the discriminatory conduct; its severity; whether it is physically threatening or humiliating, or a mere offensive utterance; and whether it unreasonably interferes with an employee's work performance," as well as any psychological harm to the plaintiff.

In concurring opinions, both Justices Antonin Scalia and Ruth Bader Ginsburg made this point more explicitly. In somewhat different ways, both said that the test was not whether a plaintiff's job performance was actually impaired, but whether the harassment had the effect of altering the working conditions in a discriminatory way.

Justice Ginsburg's brief concurring opinion was her first since she joined the Court. She appeared to go out of her way to suggest that discrimination on the basis of sex should be taken as seriously by the Court as discrimination on the basis of race, a position that she argued for as a lawyer in cases before the Court during the 1970s but that the Court has not adopted.

In a footnote, Justice Ginsburg observed that "it remains an open question" whether the Court should regard distinctions made by the Government on the basis of sex "inherently suspect," as it does for race. In making that observation, she quoted from a 1982 opinion by Justice O'Connor that declared it unconstitutional for a Mississippi state college to exclude men from a nursing program.

The decision today did not award victory to Ms. Harris but rather instructed the appeals court to reconsider the case. (Copyright © 1994 *The New York Times*)

SIMPSON CASE IS GALVANIZING U.S. ABOUT DOMESTIC VIOLENCE
By Jane Gross
Special to The New York Times

SAN FRANCISCO, July 3—Never before has the domestic violence hot line in Pacheco, Calif., been so inundated with calls for help, said Majorie Cusick, the clinical director for Battered Women's Alternatives there, and women who used to be shy and ambivalent are now "gushing" with details about their beatings and fear for their lives.

No longer are police officers falling asleep or reading newspapers at domestic-violence training sessions in San Francisco, said Ken Theisen, a paralegal at the Neighborhood Legal Assistance Foundation, who teaches classes on how to serve emergency protection orders.

Like the terrified women and the attentive officers, lawmakers and civic leaders, too, are paying new attention to domestic violence since the double murder charges against O. J. Simpson and the haunting 911 accounts of love turned to terror.

United States senators, New York State legislators and Los Angeles County supervisors, to name just a few, are scrambling to write new laws, finance new programs and take a closer look at what other localities are doing to prevent and punish an all-too-common crime, which Federal officials say is the most serious health threat to American women.

Shift in Attitudes As a trigger for social change, the Simpson case is being likened to Anita F. Hill's Senate testimony, which galvanized the nation about sexual harassment, Magic Johnson's illness, which raised consciousness about AIDS, and Polly Klaas's kidnapping, which produced a hue and cry about crime and punishment.

To be sure, it is too early to say if the national spotlight will remain fixed on the issue of domestic violence. But there is widespread agreement that attitudes have already shifted markedly.

"Sure, the attention on this issue will shift," said Donna Garske, the executive director of Marin Abused Women's Services, an agency in Northern California that counsels abused women and abusive men. "But it won't go away. You can't unblow a horn."

Calls to domestic-violence hot lines are up by as much as 80 percent in some places and generally are half again as much as they have been, officials say. "As soon as you put the phone down, it rings again," said Joan Mintz Ulner at Women Against Abuse, a Philadelphia agency.

The women seeking help now cite the 911 telephone calls made by Nicole Brown Simpson. "The fear of being killed is coming up routinely, whereas before many women wouldn't mention it," said Betty White at the Center for Women's Studies and Services Hot Line in San Diego.

Women Are Speaking Up Many women are reporting being threatened that they could wind up like Mrs. Simpson. One woman in Houston said her partner warned, "I'll do you worse than O. J. did."

But as frightened as the women are, they are less willing to remain silent. An emergency room nurse at the Graduate Health Systems City Avenue Hospital in Philadelphia said that bruised women who were brought in by men who expected them to lie about what happened were defying their mates and announcing, "He beat me; keep him away from me."

While abused women identify with that 911 call by Mrs. Simpson, men calling for help or already in treatment see themselves most vividly in Mr. Simpson's rambling, suicidal letter.

When Mr. Simpson wrote in a letter read on television that he felt like the battered partner, hurt and humiliated by his wife, men nodded and said, "That's me," said Dr. David Adams, founder of Emerge, a program for abusive men in Cambridge, Mass.

And when Mr. Simpson lamented that he loved his former wife too much, his words "struck a chord," said Denise Frey at the Women's Resource Center in San Diego, which also counsels abusive men, who are often in treatment as part of a plea agreement.

Men Are Seeking Help But since the Simpson case began, many more men not forced into treatment by a judge are asking for help with their tempers. At the House of Ruth Batterers' Program in Baltimore, for instance, 11 men came forward in just two days last week, twice the number who called in the entire previous year.

"I wouldn't call it a stampede," said Jim Denamn, director of the men's program in Pacheco, northeast of San Francisco. "But they're edging closer. They're feeling it out. They're asking, 'Is this domestic violence?' "

Lawmakers across the country and in the nation's capital sense this groundswell, and its power as an electoral issue. And they have responded with a flurry of bills and other legislative action, including the creation of a State Senate committee in Texas to research domestic violence programs in other states and millions of dollars of additional aide for shelters for battered women in Los Angeles County.

In Washington, where President Clinton last week condemned domestic violence, amendments protecting battered women were added to the crime bill now in conference committee, and lawmakers held press conferences reminiscent of those after the Anita Hill hearings promising attention to women's concerns.

In New York State, the Legislature passed an omnibus domestic violence bill on June 23 that, among other provisions, required arrests regardless of whether a woman was willing to press charges, joining 25 other states with mandatory arrest laws.

Some Innovative Programs The rush to legislate, which included several domestic violence bills in California, reminded many people of the state's hasty passage of a three-strikes-and-you're-out law after the Klaas killing. That statute was overwhelmingly endorsed by politicians of both parties, despite ample analysis of its flaws. In practice, virtually every district attorney in California agrees that the law is as misguided as predicted.

"What I fear are the knee-jerk domestic-violence laws," said Jerry Reeves, who counsels abusive men in Pacheco. "Because no one will have the courage to stand up and say, 'This is a bad idea.' "

Amid this flurry of activity, civic leaders across the nation are taking a closer look at innovative programs that have heretofore gone largely unnoticed.

The one getting the most attention is in San Diego County, where aggressive law enforcement and sophisticated treatment for offenders has led in recent years to a sharp reduction in domestic homicides and a sharp increase in convictions.

In San Diego, where 23 detectives and sergeants work full time on domestic violence cases, the largest such detail in the nation, batterers are arrested and jailed if there is any visible evidence of abuse.

Then prosecution goes forward whether or not a woman presses charges, using evidence like 911 tapes, photos, medical records and testimony from neighbors. Most batterers wind up being convicted of a misdemeanor and ordered into one of 15 court-approved treatment program. In 30 sessions over the course of a year, they discuss anger, gender roles and the like. Attendance is monitored, and drop-outs are re-arrested.

Another program that has won praise and recent attention is a domestic violence court in Dade County, Fla., where the issuance of orders of protection has increased to 9,000 a year from 4,000 a year under the administration of Judge Cindy Lederman.

Men convicted in Dade County are referred to six-month counseling programs and return to court every two months for a year. They write essays for the judges about the lessons they have learned.

Services are also supplied for family members, under a system that Judge Lederman calls "therapeutic jurisprudence." And in the interest of preventing family violence, judges visit schools to sensitize teachers and counselors and have produced a program for public television.

The difference between counties that coordinate their domestic violence programs and those that do not is readily apparent, said Rollie Mullin, the executive director of Battered Women's Alternatives in Pacheco, which serves both Contra Costa and Solano Counties.

In Contra Costa County, statistics provided by the California Department of Justice show, 22.5 percent of domestic violence arrests lead to charges and 17 percent result in convictions. In Solano County, which has a domestic violence council that meets monthly to set policy, coordinate programs and follow up cases, 66.9 percent of arrests lead to charges and 65 percent bring convictions.

"Everybody sits down at the table together there," Ms. Mullin said. "The District Attorney gets to hear how frustrated the cops are when they make an arrest and nothing happens. The cops gets to hear what kind of evidence the D.A. needs to make a case. And everybody gets to hear what the women need."

Ms. Mullin and others have urged Contra Costa County to duplicate the coordinating council that sits in the neighboring county, so far to no avail. "This could be a precipitating moment," Ms. Mullin said. "Maybe now instead of dismissing us with 'yeah, yeah, yeah,' our recommendation will bear fruit." (Copyright © 1994 *The New York Times*)

WOMEN DOING CRIME, WOMEN DOING TIME
By Clifford Krauss

Women wearing judges' robes or corporate pinstripes have become everyday images of society's changing gender roles. But what about women attired in Day-Glo prison jumpsuits?

The number of women in state and Federal prisons increased from 12,331 to 43,845 from 1980 to 1990, according to the Justice Department. That is an increase of 256 percent, compared with a 140 percent rise in the male prison population.

Arrests of women for serious felonies climbed 32.5 percent from 1988 to 1992, reaching 62,936 nationwide, according to a Justice Department canvass of more than 8,000 police agencies. The 1992 arrest figure is still small compared with the 452,453 men arrested for violent crimes that year.

The 8,000 law-enforcement agencies which responded to the canvass cover some 185 million Americans. While it does not list all people arrested in the United States, it is considered an accurate indicator of the types of crime being committed.

The fact that the rate of arrests for women under the age of 18 increased in those four years by 63 percent, compared with 45.4 percent for male youths, has attracted growing attention from law enforcement experts.

The swelling number of women being arrested and incarcerated raises questions about whether women are becoming more aggressive—in other words, more like those men who get caught up in lives of violence.

For now, a wide array of criminologists have concluded that as long as organized crime, neighborhood gangs and narcotics networks remain bastions of male domination, the answer is no, or at least not yet.

Many criminal justice scholars attribute the rise in the female crime rates more to the growing poverty among young, unattached mothers and the new ways society treats women than to the wider opportunities they have. More men are abandoning their families, leaving women with the burdens of children, and with the temptations to commit crimes to care for them.

Meanwhile, many studies find that the justice system, after decades of imposing lighter sentences, is more likely to treat wayward women harshly, be they first-time drug offenders or women who fight physically with husbands or boyfriends, even if they say the men hit them first.

"Simply put, it appears that the criminal justice system now seems more willing to incarcerate women," Meda Chesney-Lind, a University of Hawaii criminology professor, writes in a book awaiting publication.

Female criminals remain different from male wrongdoers in many respects. The percentage of women in prison for drug and property crimes is considerably higher than for male inmates. A recent study in Massachusetts, for instance, found that only 22 percent of the women imprisoned there were incarcerated for violent offenses, compared with 48 percent of the men behind bars.

Nationwide, almost two-thirds of the women in prison for violent crimes had been found guilty of assaulting or killing relatives or intimates, the Justice Department said. By contrast, violent males in prison were more than twice as likely to have assaulted or killed strangers. (But that ratio may change if the new attention being paid to spousal abuse results in more assault convictions for abusive husbands.)

Still, some argue that crimes committed by women, although far smaller in number, may nonetheless be more serious for society at large than the statistics reflect since rising rates of illegitimacy and divorce have made women even more responsible for future generations—thanks in no small measure to the irresponsibility of some men.

"Girls become mothers, and mothers influence the behaviors of their offspring," Joan McCord, a professor of criminology at Temple University, argued in an article published last year, "so that the net effects of antisocial behaviors may be greater for females than for males." A Justice Department study completed in March found that two-thirds of the women in prison have at least one child under the age of 18.

Early criminologists assumed that violence and criminal behavior were essentially masculine traits, and that the few women who did commit acts of violence suffered some sort of biological abnormality.

Caesar Lombroso, a 19th-century Italian physician, carted home bags of women's bones from the prisons of Turin to look for anatomical distinctions between criminal and noncriminal women. Lombroso's conclusion that abnormal cranium size and excessive body hair were the telltale signs of female criminal behavior were cast aside by the early 20th century.

Depicted as Deviants But the depiction of female criminals as sexual deviants persisted through the first half of the century, until most scholars concluded that criminal behavior was mostly determined by social and economic factors.

No longer was criminality a matter of testosterone. In the widely discussed book *Sisters in Crime: The Rise of the New Female Criminal* (McGraw, 1975), the criminologist Freda Adler foresaw a "rising tide of female assertiveness" that would lead tens of thousands of women to step "across the imaginary boundary line which once separated crimes into 'masculine' and 'feminine' categories."

At first glance, the increases in arrest rates of women for vehicle theft, arson, robbery and aggravated assault confirm the conclusions of the first generation of female criminologists. Just as surely as women were capable of running corporate boardrooms, they said, women who commit crimes would branch out from "traditional" offenses like prostitution and shoplifting.

If examples of this growing "diversity" are isolated, they are also chilling. Last September, a 20-year-old professional thief named Patsy Jones stung the Miami tourist industry after she was accused of fatally shooting a German tourist along the Dolphin Expressway with a sawed-off hunting rifle.

In Brooklyn recently, a teen-ager shot and killed a livery cab driver in broad daylight after he resisted her and two girlfriends during a botched robbery attempt.

But the link between changing gender models and the number of women in prison remains dubious. Female criminologists increasingly reject predictions that a female crime wave is imminent. They note that female participation in the ultimate violent crime—murder—remains extremely low.

The New York City police report that while women were accused of committing a third more felonies in 1993 than in 1975, 59 women were arrested for murder last year in the city compared with 120 women in 1975.

And while the growing number of women who work helps to explain why they are committing more forgery and embezzlement, the great majority of women in prison are poor and unemployed and not models of newly empowered, liberated women. "It's really difficult to discern whether women who commit crimes are any more liberated or have different gender-role attitudes than women who don't commit crimes," said Candace Kruttschnitt, a professor of sociology at the University of Minnesota.

"This is a murky area," she added. (Copyright © 1994 *The New York Times*)

PUSH TO REVAMP IDEAL FOR AMERICAN FATHERS
By Susan Chira

The idea of the new American father, that tender diaper-changer of the 90s, is under political attack by those who want to bring him closer to Ward Cleaver than Mrs. Doubtfire. They prescribe a provider and disciplinarian with a modern twist: he is not afraid to tell his children he loves them.

Regrouping after a foray into espousing family values and denouncing Murphy Brown, several groups ranging from conservative to centrist are mounting an ambitious public-information and political drive to combat what they call "fatherless America." They are pushing the idea that the old father, with some updating in the nurturing department, will do just fine.

The attack is occurring amid a renewed cultural and political focus on fatherhood. A flurry of legislative proposals addressing illegitimacy, welfare reform, child support and divorce law, as well as President Clinton's planned campaign against teen-age pregnancy, reflect an explosion of interest in fatherlessness.

"What we are trying to counter is this sense in our culture that the mother and father do the same thing," said Wade F. Horn, a father of two who is the director of the National Fatherhood Initiative, one of several groups trying to persuade fathers to take their responsibilities to heart. "There is a sense that if the father is not changing 50 percent of the diapers, that if a father doesn't cry frequently in front of his children, something is wrong with that father."

Long Fight by Women That message contradicts one that fathers have been hearing for years as women fought a long and painful battle to convince them that the rigid division of roles should ease as more mothers went to work and that true fatherhood lies in participating more intimately in raising children.

Proponents of the new fatherhood are rallying in defense. "These myths keep the status quo in place because we haven't yet made a full commitment to breaking them," said Dr. Ron Taffel, a father of two who wrote *Why Parents Disagree: How Women and Men Parent Differently and How We Can Work Together* (William Morrow, 1994). "The idea that Mom's in charge and Dad helps out is a flawed paradigm, and it is one of the causes of divorce and unhappy marriages"—and thus of fatherlessness.

Proponents of the new and old fatherhood agree that the United States faces a severe and growing problem: about 40 percent of American children live in households without their biological fathers. The groups part company on two issues: whether a family without a father is by definition one that is headed for trouble and whether the remedy is a renewed emphasis on traditional families.

One side argues that a father's absence is a leading cause of many of America's most vexing social problems: poverty, welfare dependency, crime and failure in school. Mr. Horn and his colleagues believe that fathers bring something irreplaceable and inherently masculine to a family: qualities like discipline, risk-taking and decisiveness that are the hallmarks of the traditional father.

Advertisements Planned Several groups, including Mr. Horn's, say they plan an all-out drive through public-service advertisements and grass-roots organizing to promote responsible fatherhood and to ask individual fathers to pledge their commitment to their children.

They believe that society should discourage unwed fatherhood and divorce, and they want all fathers—married, unwed or divorced—to fulfill their responsibilities to their children. And while they urge fathers to become more involved in their children's lives, they fear that some of the emphasis on blurring the roles of mother and father has conned people into believing that families will do fine without fathers.

"Ultimately, the revival of fatherhood implies challenging some of the premises of the sexual revolution and of radical feminism," said William Kristol, the director of the Project for the Republican Future, who was an aide to Dan Quayle when he was Vice President. He said he saw echoes in this debate of many ideas that Mr. Quayle was mocked for embracing.

Consider these excerpts from the literature of the National Fatherhood Initiative:

"At times of crisis or stress, the traditionally male values—especially the ability to contain emotions and be decisive—are invaluable."

"Father encourages risk taking. Mother encourages caution."

"When a child has difficulty at school, a family car is wrecked, or a dispute with a creditor arises, it is often the father who confronts the issue."

Even many of the most ardent proponents of a more involved and sensitive fatherhood say they do not think that fathers and mothers are the same or play identical roles in the family. But they see this newest drive as reinforcing outmoded stereotypes.

"Fathers and mothers do have different styles, but there's a tendency to confuse those differences with things that are much more essential," said Dr. James Levine, a father of two and the director of the Fatherhood Project in New York, a program that works to involve fathers of all income levels with their children. "Kids need continuous care, a sense somebody believes in them, a sense of hope for the future." These, he said, can be supplied by either parent.

It is not yet clear how these two views of fatherhood are playing outside the think-tank circuit. Most men never really bought the idea of the new father. Study after study shows that mothers, even if they are working full time and bringing home paychecks at least equal to the fathers', still do most child-rearing and household chores.

But many people also seemed to reject the "family values" crusade of the 1992 Republican National Convention, and politicians quickly dropped that theme after being labeled intrusive and intolerant. Mr. Horn, a clinical psychologist who served as the Commissioner of Children, Youth and Families under President George Bush, is careful to distance himself from some of the views of the far right.

"A lot of people interpret this as an attack on single motherhood," Mr. Horn said, "and that's not what it's about. Anybody, whether a single mother or a father, trying to raise a family deserves everyone's support and encouragement, not their scorn and condemnation. Still, it does nobody any good, least of all children, to say fathers are unimportant."

Matters of Fear and Guilt Yet, Dr. Levine said he believed that much of the debate ended up compounding the fear and guilt of single mothers and attacking the existence of diverse families, including those headed by lesbians.

David G. Blankenhorn, the author of *Fatherless America*, to be published by Basic Books, is the father of a son and one of the most tireless promoters of bringing back a more traditional view of fatherhood.

"My criticism of the new father paradigm is that it acts as if the only act worth crediting is nurture," said Mr. Blankenhorn, who is also president of the Institute for American Values, a research organization in New York, and the chairman of the National Fatherhood Initiative. "But the deep meaning of masculinity for most men is the idea of providing for and teaching children, and that should be celebrated."

Mr. Blankenhorn said that several studies of parent-child interactions had shown that fathers tended to roughhouse while mothers tended to comfort, and that fathers tended to assume the role of coach, teacher and enforcer of standards.

Differences Not Innate But these differences are not necessarily innate or inevitable.

"Children talk in the midst of doing other things, when someone is giving them a bath," Dr. Taffel said. "The one who does more of that is the one who finds more out. It's not inborn; it just happens to be that women happen to do more of that."

Mr. Blankenhorn and Mr. Horn said that they were not trying to revive the 1950s father nor redraw traditional sexual roles, but rather to curb what they saw as excesses of feminism and to reward fathers for their contributions.

"We are not about turning the clock back," Mr. Horn said. "This initiative is not about moving back to the 1950s stereotype of the cold and distant martinet father who was afraid to say 'I love you' to his kids. That was very destructive, and men found that unfulfilling. But it is equally oppressive to say that men will not become new fathers unless they do half the diaper changes or bottle feedings." (Copyright © 1994 *The New York Times*)

PENTAGON MUST REINSTATE NURSE WHO DECLARED SHE IS A LESBIAN
By Eric Schmitt
Special to The New York Times

WASHINGTON, June 1—A Federal judge in Seattle ordered the military today to reinstate a highly decorated nurse who was forced out of the Washington State National Guard after acknowledging that she is a lesbian.

The judge, Thomas S. Zilly of Federal District Court, ordered Col. Margarethe Cammermeyer back to the job she held in 1992, ruling that the military's policy on homosexuals at that time was based solely on prejudice and was a clear violation of the Constitution's equal-protection clause.

At a hastily convened news conference in Seattle today, Colonel Cammermeyer beamed with delight and told reporters: "I feel a little bit like a general who has won a war. There is exoneration."

Judge Zilly's decision dealt with the Pentagon's old policy on homosexuals, not the new regulations that Congress and the Clinton Administration agreed on last year. The new rules permit homosexuals in the military as long as they remain silent about their sexual orientation.

But the new "don't ask, don't tell, don't pursue" rules share many similarities with the old ones, and the Administration is defending the old policy in court to set precedents that would make challenges to the new policy more difficult. Judge Zilly is the latest of several Federal judges to find the old policy unconstitutional, raising concern in the Administration that the same analysis could be applied to the new policy.

Pentagon officials said tonight that they were reviewing Judge Zilly's decision and considering whether to appeal.

Gay-rights advocates today hailed the ruling as one of a growing number of Federal court challenges to the old policy that, collectively, could cut away at the undergirding of both old and new rules.

"This is yet another statement from the courts that they're looking at the constitutionality of this policy, and it's failing the test," said William Rubenstein, director of the American Civil Liberties Union's Lesbian and Gay Rights Project.

Indeed, Judge Zilly struck at a basic assumption in the old and the new policy: that homosexual orientation signifies an intent to engage in homosexual conduct. The judge concluded "there is no rational basis for the Government's underlying contention that homosexual orientation equals 'desire or propensity to engage' in homosexual conduct."

Judge Zilly ordered the National Guard to expunge any record of Colonel Cammermeyer's sexual orientation in order to prevent the military from taking any further action against her when she returns to service.

While Federal district judges around the country have shown some support for striking down the ban on homosexuals, appeals courts are only just beginning to consider the cases. In the next few years, these cases are ultimately expected to reach the United States Supreme Court, which would have the final say.

Sympathy of Commanders The United States Courts of Appeals for the District of Columbia Circuit and for the Ninth Circuit, which covers nine Western states, are two of the most important appeals courts in the country and both are expected to issue decisions in the next few months.

Colonel Cammermeyer's case drew special attention because of the way the military discovered she was homosexual and the widespread support among her commanders to ignore the ban and let her stay on duty.

Even Senator Sam Nunn, the Georgia Democrat who championed the move on Capitol Hill to maintain restrictions on openly gay service members, expressed sympathy with Colonel Cammermeyer's plight.

During a top-secret security clearance review in 1989 that was required for admission to the Army War College, Colonel Cammermeyer was asked about her sexual orientation, and she told the interviewer she was gay. Under the Administration's new policy, that question is no longer asked. And if it was, she would not be required to answer.

But under the old policy, her statement was ground for discharge. Even so, Colonel Cammermeyer's superiors at the Washington State National Guard told her she could continue to serve as the guard's chief nurse unless the Army Department pressed the issue.

Bronze Star and More Indeed, Colonel Cammermeyer's record was the stuff of recruiting posters. When she was a child, her family fled the Nazis after they invaded her native Norway in World War II. After coming to the United States, she joined the Army as a nurse in 1961.

She was awarded the Bronze Star after serving 15 months in Vietnam, supervising a hospital for wounded and dying soldiers. In 1985, she was chosen from 34,000 candidates nationwide as the Veterans Administration's Nurse of the Year.

Colonel Cammermeyer, who is 52, served as chief nurse for three years after she admitted her homosexuality, while military review boards debated her fate. Gov. Booth Gardner of Washington appealed to Defense Secretary Dick Cheney to retain Colonel Cammermeyer.

But on June 11, 1992, Colonel Cammermeyer was dismissed with an honorable discharge, apparently becoming the highest-ranking officer to be discharged solely because of homosexual orientation. At the Washington National Guard headquarters, Colonel Cammermeyer wept, as did her commanding officer, Maj. Gen. Gregory P. Barlow. She then vowed to fight the military's ban.

Fear as Basis for Policy She was vindicated, at least for now, in Judge Zilly's ruling. "The Government has discriminated against Colonel Cammermeyer solely on the basis of her status as a homosexual and has failed to demonstrate a rational basis for doing so," the judge wrote in a 51-page ruling.

Judge Zilly, who was appointed by President Ronald Reagan, noted that military experts "conceded that their justifications for the policy are based on heterosexual members' fear and dislike of homosexuals." He added, "Mere negative attitudes, or fear, are constitutionally impermissible bases for discriminatory governmental policies."

Since her discharge, Colonel Cammermeyer has worked as a clinical specialist at a Veterans Administration hospital in Tacoma, Wash. She has also written a book on her experience that is to be published in October by Viking.

In a telephone interview, Colonel Cammermeyer said that, barring an appeal by the Government, she was looking forward to continuing her work at the Veterans Administration hospital, but in her old National Guard rank. "I have no reservations about going back, but I know I'll have butterflies," she said. (Copyright © 1994 *The New York Times*)

WOMEN IN COLOMBIA MOVE TO JOB FOREFRONT
By James Brooke
Special to The New York Times

BOGOTA, Columbia—In 1933, the fathers of this country grudgingly agreed to a novel experiment by allowing a woman to enroll in a Colombian university. Six decades later, women outnumber men in the universities, 52 percent to 48 percent.

In the mid-1960s, ignoring opposition from the quasi-official Roman Catholic Church, social workers started to introduce family planning. Three decades later, the average Colombian woman has 2.7 children, about one-third the 1964 level of 7.4.

Breaking stereotypes, Colombian women have marched out of the home and into the labor force with startling velocity. With greater education, fewer children and a realization that a man will not necessarily always be around to provide, Colombian women of all classes are aggressively pursuing a financial independence unthinkable before.

"In Colombia, there is a great family crisis," said Maruja Pachon de Villamizar, the nation's Education Minister. "Women have entered the universities and the work force, but men don't understand the new roles."

Independence for Women Until recently, Leonor Montoya Alvarez, the president of Banco de Colombia, the country's largest commercial bank, said: "I no longer run into girls who say they want to marry well and never work. Having economic independence is part of a Colombian woman's self-esteem."

"In most bank branches now, it's 'la gerente,' " Ms. Montoya said, using the feminine version of a Spanish word for manager. "Today, 30 to 50 percent of people at a bank meeting will be women."

Overall in Latin America, women make up one-third of the labor force, double the proportion of a generation ago. But in Colombia's cities, women's share of the work force rose during the same period from one-third to 43 percent.

"At the turn of the century, a Colombian women had three choices: get married at 16, enter a convent, or become an old maid," said Ximena Pachon, an anthropologist here. "Today, the possibilities are immense. That's why you see a day-care center on every block in Bogota."

An Increasing Program Ciudad Bolivar, a sprawling working-class neighborhood in Bogota, is dotted with "community homes," government-financed centers that provide day care and meals for up to 15 children under the age of 7 in one home. Devised to allow poor women to hold down jobs, Colombia's community home network has mushroomed across the country in recent years, increasing the number of children under care from 115,000 in 1987 to 1.7 million today.

Colombian social scientists argue that women in this country of 36 million people are tougher and more independent than women elsewhere in South America. This toughness, they say, is forged by the country's demanding, mountainous terrain, and by a male homicide rate that makes young widowhood common.

With murder the leading cause of violent death for men, Colombia had a homicide rate last year of 79 murders per 100,000 people, seven times the United States rate. In Colombia's two largest cities, Bogota and Medellin, the homicide rate is twice Colombia's national average. Last year, Ana Rico de Alonso, a sociologist, directed a study of Muzo, an Andean emerald mining community 100 miles north of here where violence left 40 percent of households headed by women.

"Children drew pictures of their families," she recounted. "Not one woman was depicted carrying out a household chore. They were shown farming, mining or tending cattle."

Households Headed by Women A world away from the emerald wars, Bogota, a capital city of eight million people, also has 40 percent of households headed by women. By comparison, the proportion is 17 percent in Sao Paulo, South America's largest city.

One prominent biologist here recalled that after she appeared on a list of Colombia's 10 most influential women, her husband stopped talking to her for three months. Then, he divorced her, a procedure that was legalized in Colombia only last year.

Aware that they may have to fend for themselves, Colombian women of all classes increasingly seek financial independence. And in Ciudad Bolivar, Bogota's largest poor neighborhood, women entrepreneurs are increasingly gaining control of their own finances.

"It's not that we only wanted to work with women, but women are more serious—they meet their obligations," said Nelly Garcia, who with three other female business partners runs a business sewing brightly colored nylon bicycle backpacks.

Criticism of Husbands Down a few twisting hillside alleys, Briceda Guioth de Espinosa bustled around a tiny corner store that she opened "after my husband took off five years ago."

"We didn't want any men in our group," Mrs. Guioth said of her business partnership. "They drink their loans, they don't work their stores. Why should we have to pay for their irresponsibilities? One man joined, but he had to submit to our rules."

Down the hill, at the headquarters of the bank that makes small-business loans, Jose Antonio Jaime scanned a computerized ledger.

"The ladies are better with the payments," said Mr. Jaime, who manages the loan program, which is affiliated with Accion International, a small-business promotion organization based in Cambridge, Mass. "Statistics show that the women are more organized and more punctual."

Machismo vs. Marketing He said that in a country where high school boys have a higher dropout rate than girls, working-class Colombian men often fall victim to their own machismo.

"Typically, the man doesn't want to go to the classes, so he sends his wife," he said of small business courses offered to his program's 32,000 participants. "After a while, the wife starts talking about rotation of inventory, marketing efficiency, profit margins. Pretty soon, the wife has taken over the business—all because of the husband's machismo."

In part, Colombian women have greater economic independence, because they have greater control over child birth. About two-thirds of fertile age Colombian women use some form of contraception, one of the world's highest rates. Despite Catholic opposition and half-hearted Government crackdowns, about 400,000 abortions are performed in Colombia each year. Recent surveys indicate that 3.4 percent of all fertile-age Colombian women have an abortion each year, compared with 2.7 percent for women in the United States.

This year, Colombia has started a nationwide sex education program, obligatory for all ninth graders. Devoted more to postponing sex than explaining it, the program is a pioneer for South America.

More Enrollments "With the family-planning programs, the implicit message to women all over the country was: if you have fewer children, you can do more with your life," said Ms. de Alonso, the sociologist. "And that is what happened."

Although women's salaries generally lag 30 percent behind men's salaries, future expansion of women in business seems guaranteed by university enrollments. Twenty years ago, for every Colombian woman studying economics or business administration, there were three men. Today, the ratio is 1 to 1. In engineering, long a male preserve, the ratio has dropped in half, to one woman student for every three men.

But despite growing financial clout, Colombian women have been slow to win commensurate political power. In 1954, they were given the vote and allowed to run for office. Four decades later, 47 percent of voters are women, but only 10 percent of elective offices are held by women.

Many of today's successful women in the work force say they were inspired to go into business or public service when Belisario Betancourt, a conservative President in the 1970s, reserved all his deputy ministerial positions for women. Today, several high-profile Colombian women are also providing role models to a new generation of Colombian girls.

A Popular Leader Ana Milena Munoz, wife of Colombia's President, Cesar Gaviria Trujillo, has charted a public role along the lines of Hillary Rodham Clinton. Colombia's first First Lady with a degree in economics, she has a university-trained staff, an office, and a strong voice over state social and cultural spending.

Noemi Sanin de Rubio has been so popular as Foreign Minister that the two leading presidential candidates fell over each other in March trying, in vain, to persuade her to run for Vice President. "We would have won the first time if Noemi had been on our ticket," said an adviser to one candidate. (Copyright © 1994 *The New York Times*)

Discussion Questions

1. Do you think that discrimination against women will be easier or harder to eradicate than discrimination against racial and ethnic minorities?

2. Are male attitudes and behaviors the only reason why women continue to experience discrimination and prejudice?

3. Do you think that women ought to be allowed to play combat roles in the military and to serve as priests in the Catholic Church? Discuss.

4. The past two decades have seen dramatic changes in American gender roles. What have men, women, and the society as a whole gained as a result of these changes? What have we lost?

5. Do you think that gays and lesbians ought to be protected by antidiscrimination legislation? Why?